D0240292

TRUMP
RANT

About the Author

Chris Agee is a poet, essayist, photographer and editor. He was born in San Francisco on a US Navy hospital ship and grew up in Massachusetts, New York and Rhode Island. After high school at Phillips Academy Andover and a year in Aix-en-Provence, France, he attended Harvard University and since graduation has lived in Ireland. His third collection of poems, *Next to Nothing* (Salt, 2008), was shortlisted in Britain for the 2009 Ted Hughes Award for New Work in Poetry, and its sequel, *Blue Sandbar Moon* (The Irish Pages Press), appeared in 2018. He is the Editor of *Irish Pages*, and edited *Balkan Essays* (The Irish Pages Press, 2016), the sixth volume of Hubert Butler's essays, published simultaneously in Croatian by the Zagreb publishing house Fraktura. He lives in Belfast, and divides his time between Ireland, Scotland and Croatia.

On *Blue Sandbar Moon:*

"I think it is a monumental work ranging
across both the European landscape
and the deepest inner worlds."

David Park, *novelist*

TRUMP RANT

CHRIS AGEE

THE IRISH PAGES PRESS
2021

Trump Rant
is first published in hardback
on 18 January 2021.

The Irish Pages Press
129 Ormeau Road
Belfast BT7 1SH
Ireland

www.irishpages.org

Legal Advice: Flynn O'Driscoll, Dublin

Typeset in 14/18 pt Monotype Perpetua
Designed and composed by RV, Belfast. Printed by Bell & Bain, Glasgow.

A CIP catalogue record for this book
is available from The British Library.

Dust-jacket images: "Death on the Ridge Road" by Grant Wood
and author photograph by Keith Lang.

ISBN: 978-0-9935532-9-5

Also by Chris Agee

POETRY

In the New Hampshire Woods
(1992)

First Light
(2003)

Next to Nothing
(2008)

Blue Sandbar Moon
(2018)

AS EDITOR

Scar on the Stone: Contemporary Poetry from Bosnia
(1998)

Unfinished Ireland: Essays on Hubert Butler
(2003)

The New North: Contemporary Poetry from Northern Ireland
(2008)

The Other Tongues: An Introduction to Writing in Irish, Scots Gaelic and Scots in Ulster and Scotland
(2013)

Balkan Essays
by Hubert Butler
(2016)

CONTENTS

For Jacob and Ciarán

After Allen Ginsberg
(Poetry or prose: take your pick)

MIDTERM REPORT

(2017 – 2019)

Trump Is Mob Culture
Trump Likes Interpersonal Power
Trump Makes Enemies
Trump Mocks
Trump Is New York
Trump Loves the East
Trump Hates Change
Trump Is a Grifter
Trump Is Impermeable
Trump Never Laughs

Trump Loves Ranting
Trump Is Simple-minded But Foxy/FOXy
Trump Is All Subtext
Trump Is Annoying Coin-operated American
    Airport Cart
Trump Verbalizes
Trump Lies
Trump Leverages (People Too)
Trump Bullies
Trump Is the System Gone South
Trump Is Lazy
Trump Was/Is Bankrupt
Trump Is Wild and Crazy Guy
Trump Neither Cares Nor Empathizes
Trump Is a Cultural Freak
Trump Controls Body Language of Others
Trump Is a Throwback
Trump Is Always the Victim
Trump Is an Asshole
Trump Is the Shrimp-salad Now
Trump Likes McDonald's
Trump Has Mussolini Issues
Trump Is a Drama Queen
Trump Is Not New But Old
Trump Is a Copperhead (Natural and Historical)
Trump Is the Duke-and-King Con in
    Huckleberry Finn

Trump Is American Weird
Trump Is Frozen Adolescent Syndrome
Trump Is a Self-confessed Philanderer
Trump Is Pharaonic: Like Robert Moses
Trump Was a Square
Trump Is Pure Indulgence
Trump Is a Daddy's Boy
Trump Is Patriarchy
Trump Likes Pre-feminist Eastern Women
Trump Likes Israel's Ethno-state (Arabs As Blacks)
Trump Is Faustian
Trump Is Faux Protestant
Trump Is the Defenestration of Decency
Trump Issued Fake Certificates
Trump Likes His Name on Towels
Trump Is Worse Than Bibi
Trump Loves Combover
Trump Is the Republic's Mephistopheles
Trump Is a Catastrophe
Trump Is *We the Mob*
Trump Is Insecure
Trump Speaks No Languages (Not Even English)
Trump Is the Jackass in The White House
Trump Hates Being "One-upped"
(Like in Northern Ireland)
Trump Is Colossal Brittle Ego
Trump Is Angry Man

Trump Hates Change (Post-'68)
Trump Wants It All Back
Trump Is Ungreat Gatsby
Trump Loves Spectacle
Trump Is Spectacle
Trump Loves Tacky Spectacle
Trump Is Empty
Trump Is Vast Carelessness

Trump Is the Corrupted Dream
Trump Is Bankrupt in Every Sense
Trump Is Common American Insular
Trump Is Ignorant International Filter-bubble
Trump Prefers (Like "Talented Mr Ridley")
a Fake Somebody To a Real Nobody
Trump Is Dr Jekyll (POTUS) and Mr Hyde (Twitter)
Trump Is Two-faced
Trump Loves Nicknames
Trump Is Dangerous Bullshit
Trump Just Believes What He Says at Any Moment
Trump Flatters and Uses Flattery
Trump Bamboozles
Trump Is Highly Complex As a Type
Trump Must Be Centre-stage Regardless
Trump Ingratiates
Trump Likes Outsmarting

Trump Is Snake Oil
Trump Flourishes
Trump Glories
Trump Struts Like a Cockerel, or a Cock
Trump Struts and Preens (Like a Queen)
Trump Is Political Drag
Trump Is the Moment
Trump Is Pure Ego
Trump Loves Libel As Self-revelation
Trump Is Nasty Agency
Trump Is Interest Figurehead (on Ship of State)
Trump Bluffs by Bluster
Trump Is Ranting Gossip
Trump Is Effeminate
Trump Loves the Sound of Himself
Trump Is Queens Vernacular
Trump Is a Joe Pesci Guy
Trump Is Non-Mob Goodfella
Trump Is *Culture First*
Trump Fakes Fake News
Trump Makes Fake News
Trump Is American *Duce*
Trump Is Logorrhoea
Trump Fills His Void With *Talk Talk Talk*
Trump Is Quick-witted Corner Boy Vernacular
Trump Is the Old American Urban Street
Trump Is Transgressive

Trump Is Proto-Duterte
Trump Needs Bleiburg
Trump Has Many Mussolini-like Stage Gestures
Trump Is Vicious
Trump Is Radical Right Élite
Trump Has Perfect Feel For Political Trigger Points
Trump Is a True Performer
Trump Is Deadly Serious Political Stand-up
Trump Is Far From Buffoon Boris
Trump Loves the Royal *We*
Trump Has the Knack of Making His Crowd a *We*
Trump Needs *They* For His *We*
Trump Loves To Mock
Trump Is Master Sycophant
Is Trump Iago?
Trump Is a Real Wrecking Ball
Trump Is Trumpery
Trump Is Pure Self-trumpet
Trump Is Pure Self-interest
Trump Radically Cleaves So-called Street From
So-called Political Class
Trump Needs Taking Down
Trump Is Not WASP
Trump Loves Tacky
Trump Mis-sees, Misestimates His Hairstyle
and Suntan
Trump Is Corrupted

Trump Is Dangerous Will To Power
Trump Has Roots in American Nativist Hatred
of Europe
Trump Like Putin Uses Chaos As a Tactic
Trump Is The Great Confusion
Trump Brooks No Advice
Trump Is Not *Eye* But *Storm*
Trump Is King of Something Known To Himself
Trump Is Rump of Dead America
Trump Is True White Trash
Trump Has No Control
Trump Is Legal Mob
Trump Is Whitewasher
Trump Is Bernie Madoff With Lawyer-bagman

Trump Is
Trump Is Tribal
Trump Dictates Screeds For Others
Trump Bulldozes Everything Before Him
Trump Is Fearful (Both Senses)
Trump Is Child-abusing Barrage of Contradiction
(Mexican Border)
Trump Wants Libertarian Playground For Oligarchs
Trump Wants Manipulated/Manipulative
Semi-democracy at Best

Trump Does Not Want a Powerful Liberal West
With High Legal Standards on Which
It Depends
Trump Does Not Want Clean Law Enforcement
Trump Wants Corruption Over FBI
Trump Loves Above All Power
Trump Is The Great Realignment
Trump Is Simply Angry White Man
(With Arm Candy)
Trump Treats the Nation Like a Crappy Country
Trump Smells a Dying International Order
Trump Thinks He Has Taken Control
of the Constitutional Firm
Trump Is Typical (If *Outré* and Wild) American
Temperament
Trump Is Ruled by Slights and Anger
Trump Is "Insecurity Forces"
Trump Is the Culmination of Colin Woodard's
"New Netherland"

Trump Is a Thin-skinned Twat
Trump's Self-love Thinks Others Must Naturally
Love Him
Trump Is a Panglossian-dystopian American Psycho
Trump Prefers Oligarchs, Autocrats and Bimbos
(Both Sexes)

Trump's "Southern White House" Is Subtext/Code
For Jefferson Davis
Trump Is Simple-minded Show
Trump Really Has Missed That Part of Life Called
"Intellect"
Trump Like Kim Is *Burger Boy*
Trump's Praise Is Like Deadly Mob Charm
Trump's Real Time Is Actually and Essentially
Media-time
Trump Has No Long-term
Trump Is "HyperNormalisation"
Trump Is, Thus, the System's *Lobotomy of Consciousness*
Trump Is Westchester Without Consequences
(As Usual)
Trump Is Heading For It
Trump Is a Fucked-up Human Being
Trump Has Launched a Civic Civil War

And me?

For every Copperhead
There is a Tennessee Volunteer

Viva *Candide!*

Trump Is Directionless Spectacle
Trump's Words Are All Surface Veneer
Trump Is Cuckoo in the NATO Nest
Trump Is Anything But "One-dimensional"
(Lionel Shriver)
Trump Is Deadly Ignorance-cum-arrogance
Trump Has No Learning Resources
Trump Is Seventh-grade USA
Trump Is High-class Tat
Trump Is "Pulp Fiction" *Sans* Tarantino Intelligence
Trump Is a Mouth Who Loves Mouthing
Trump Cannot Distinguish Really Between
Self and Policy
Trump's Trumpery Has Something of the
Effeminate Unbuttoned Gossip
Trump Is Teenaged Callow
Trump Has Incredible Ego and Gall
Trump Likes To Be Liked
Trump Likes To Be Hated
Trump's Words Are Meaningless
Trump Lacks Real Meaning
Trump Is Fake Meaning
Trump Is Verbalization in a Void (*à la* NYC)
Trump Is a Panglossian Hobbes,
or a Hobbesian Pangloss
Trump Is Nasty, Brutish and Non-short

Trump Is Oleaginous As a Mob Coven
Trump Is Dementedly Transparent
Trump Is Stuck

Trump Is Lazy-primitive
Trump Is Pure Shamelessness
Trump Is Both Denialism and Post-denialism
Trump Is Loser and Abuser
Trump Is Momentary
Trump's Confidence Derives From Interpersonal
        Power Success

Trump Is Straight/Square Wicca
Trump's Brain Runs on the Pure Oxygen of
        Oxymoron
Trump Is a Stain
Trump Is the Real Plot Against America
Trump Is Always a Whirlwind
Trump Is the Arrogance of Ignorance
Trump Has the Permanent Bad-boy Syndrome
Trump Is a Deadly Serious Laughingstock
Trump Lacks Even the Idea of Self-discipline/
        Self-control
Trump Is Unhinged American Boosterism
Trump Is Trumped Up

Trump Morphs Before a Crowd
Trump Lives in the Moment Always
Trump Is Two-faced: Like a True Mobster
Trump Revels in Grandiosity
Trump Is Continually Unresolved Cognitive
Dissonance
Trump Is Vicious Character Assassination
Trump Is a Villain
Trump Lacks Interest
Trump Is Salesman Pure and Simple
Trump Is the Wolf of Washington
Trump Can Be "Funny" (and "Funny Funny")
Trump Is a Ham
Trump Inhabits Trumpistan
Trumptalk Uses Talk As Continual Self-comfort

Trump's New York Thing Is Totally Uninhibited
Freedom and Speech
Trump Can Be Funny Like a Goodfella
Trump Is a Monster
Trump Is Yonkers Living in Bronxville
Trump Hardly Knows What He Thinks
Trump Is Inauthentic Authentic
Trump Says One Thing and Does Another
Trump Leads the Era of Doublespeak
Trump Is Blue-collar Culture Enriched

Trump Enflames and Dampens
Trump's Mixed Messages Win Over Waverers
With Plausible Deniability
Trump's Verbal Diarrhea Is Unmoored Filler
Trump Lacks the Intelligence To See
the Level of His Thought and Speech
Trump Is a Hothead
Trump Is Rotten Freedom
Trump Is a Dimwit Doctor Faustus
Trump Is Not Interested in Solutions Over Pandering
Trump Belittles As Divider-in-Chief
Trump Is the Absence of Governance
Trump Wishes To End Civil Governance
Trump Is Improvised President,
Unwilling To Be Educated

Trump Has Greaser Hair
Trump Is My School Bully, Chipper Whiting
Trump Has a Tacky Tan

Trump Makes Nice When He Wants Something
Trump Makes Nasty When Thwarted
Trump's Chaos Uses Power To Hide His Ineptitude
Compared To Subordinates
Trump Likes Unmediated Action and Power

Trump Is Highly Volatile, Fleeting and Fickle
Trump Is Full of Grudges, Paranoia and Vengeance:
PPD?
Trump's Tweets Are His Id, His Office-talk His Ego

Trump Is a Wanker
Trump Is Prissy and Flitty

Trump Is a (Snake-oil) Revolutionary
Trump Is The Confidence Man
Trump, *Catch Me If You Can*
Trump Uses "Fake" Because He Is Fake
With His Fake CV
Trump Is Obnoxious
Trump's True Vice: an Aversion To Reading
Trump Can't Think
Trump Is a Madman Huckster
Trump's Decisions Centre Mob-like Around
Interpersonal Power Acts, Not Actual Policy

Trump Is Delusional-plausible
Trump Is Consistent in His Inconsistency
Trump's Verbal Diarrhoea Is Feeling Good About
Himself in the Moment

Trump's Verbal Diarrhoea Masks the Dry Heaves of His Intellect
Trump's "Decisions" Always Involve Intensely Personal and Immediate Political Circumstances
Trump Is Verbally Maladroit, Physically Awkward, and Deeply Weird
Trump Is, in a Nutshell, an Insecure Headcase

Fuck you, Trump!

Viva *Voltaire!*

THIRD-YEAR ADDENDUM: TRUMPS AND MORE TRUMPS

(2019 – 2020)

Trump Will Be Trumped by Political and
Cultural Gravity
Trump Is Expert at Deflection and Distraction
Trump Is Lazy, Pure and Simple
Trump Like Boris Speaks To the Supreme Danger
of Unbridled Self-belief

Trump Is a Brat
Trump Is Out of His Depth
Trump Uses Mob Techniques To Issue
Deniable Orders (Cohen)
Trump Was Really Formed in the Wild West *Mores*
of the Cultural Seventies
Trump Is Out of Control
Trump's Dawn Twitter Incontinence Reveals a
Simple and Immature Mind Despite the
Learnt Verbal Stream of Diarrhoea and Its
Apparent Lip-gloss
Trump Is a Toxic Dump
Trump Is Self-anointed
Trump Is Unstable Enough To End Up in a
Hitlerian Bunker
Trump Has Animal Smarts
Trump Is an Intuitive Showman
Trump Means by "Good" and "Bad" People
"Loyal" and "Disloyal"

Trump's Tweets and Comments Suggest That He Is
in Constant Incoherent Emotional Chaos
Trump Simply Has No Control, Filter, Check or Veto
Concerning the Thought-language Conduit
Trump's Use of ALL CAPITAL TWEETS Bespeaks
Unaware Childish Immaturity
Trump Suffers From Victimology and
a Limitless Persecution Complex
Trump at "News" "Conferences" Combines Deep
Uber-authoritarianism, Insults,
Conspiracy Theories, Complete Deafness
To Conversational Norms,
and a Brittle American Gentility
Trump Will Lash Out in Danger, Like a Wounded Rat
Trump's Use of Nuclear Codes Cannot and
Could Not Be Stopped by the Military
Once Activated by the Black Box
Trump Uses Conspiracy Theories (Birther, Biden)
When Facts Challenge His Politico-cultural
Belief System
Trump in the End Will Be Defeated by That Literate
Collective Global Power Known As
"The Study"
Trump Actually Used the Phrase Made Famous
by the Psycho in *Taxi Driver*:
"Are you talking to me?"

Trump's Use of Mobtalk ("Good", "Bad", "Nice", "Beautiful") Is Perforce Infused With Criminal Groupthink
Trump Is Simply an Incredibly Nasty Algorithm Comprised of All These Algebraic Variables
Trump Is In-credible *Per Se*
Trump Emerges From "New Netherland" As Described Precisely in Woodard's *American Nations*

Trump's Ego Fills All His Space
Trump's Transference Is Achieved Through Mudslinging
Trump Scores Very High on Ronson's Psychopathic Test
Trump Plays "Top Trumps" With the Whole World
Trump Loves "More Trumps"
Trump Like All Dictators Thinks Himself Into *I Am The People*
Trump's Mudfights Aim To Level Opponents To His Level
Trump Is Off-piste With the Most Basic Facts of Geography and Physiology
Trump Is King of a Certain Cultural Underclass
Trump Is the *Maestro* of Unfounded Obsessions and Confirmation Biases

Trump Lacks the Background Reading Structure
To Frame His Purely Oral/Aural Formation
Trump Is The Great Mischief-maker,
The Grand Spoiler
Trump's Self-belief Structure Trumps
Any Other Belief-structure
Trump's Transference of Personal Mud, Opaque To
Himself, Works on His Mud-splattered
Cynical Base
Trump's Language – "Great and Unmatched
Wisdom", "Destroy and Obliterate" –
Suggests a Conduit Between Emotion and
Words Gone Haywire and Tenuous
Trump's "Kurd-Normandy" Parallel Is Typical of
His Ludicrous Mobster Logic
Trump Is a Dark Clown True To the Duke and
King in Twain's *Huckleberry Finn*:
Something Old in America, Bombast of the
Confidence Trick, Allowed by the Frontier
and Its Suckers

Trump Has No Real Causes: It's All in the Glorious,
Stirring Moment, Like a Fix
Trump Must *Make America Great Again* by Dealing
and Pimping To Those Who Must Be Made
First To Denigrate It

Trump Lacks the Charm of "Many an Irish Rogue"
Trump Fixes on a False Fact So He Can Forget
the (Troubling) Issue
Trump Perforce Accuses the Dems of His Own
Corruptions, Crimes and Misdemeanors
Trump Is Transparently Guilty of the
Unauthorized Use of Songs
Trump Is Tokenistic
Trump Makes Use of Gangsta Blacks Hated by
Most African Americans
(Including My Nephews)
Trump's Accusations Are Largely Self-accusations,
Even Self-reflections

Trump Is Trumpeted by Trumpists
Trump Is Unfit For Nuclear Codes
Trump Is Instinctively Stupid
Trump Repeats Words and Phrases in
Rapid Succession As Filler For
His Know-nothing Mind
Trump Illustrates Perfectly the Adage of an
Ancient Chinese General: *Tactics Without
Strategy Are the Noise Before Defeat*
Trump Is a Person Who Understands Only His Own
Niche or Statue Space, Which He Fills With
His Pygmalion Ego

Trump's Behaviour Constantly Raises the Question: *Quo Vadis?*

Trump Seems To Feel That by Just Saying It, He Can Create It: a True *Production of Deconstruction?*

Trump's Signature Reminds Me of Hitler's, Above All in the Apparent Obliviousness To the Parallel

Trump's Narcissistic Spin Flows From a Deep Boosterism Characteristic of American "Advancement"

Trump Shows Signs of Nero Degeneration

Trump Has No Felt Understanding of Law Over Power

Trump Has No Sense of the Tapestry of History, Just a Few Threadbare Threads

Trump's Confidence Trickery Means *Showdown* and *Letdown* Are Two Sides of the Same Coinage

Trump Is Pure Entitlement

Trumpspeak's Letter To Erdogan Bespeaks Both Tabloid Mobspeak and a Profound Distance From the Actual Experience of Writing and Its Usual Mental Conventions

Trump's Hatred of Experts and Establishments Is a Field-day For His Unbridled Ego

Trump Has No Real Understanding of What *Nothing Wrong* Means

Trump's One Achievement Is To Disintegrate
Neo-liberal Hubris With His Own
Narcissism
Trump Might Just Have a "Personality Disorder"
Deep Down, Given His Obsessions,
Like Reading About Himself
Trump Might Be Depressed Under All
the Noise and Spiel
Trump Is Totally Ignorant Under All the Pseudo-
plausible Verbalizing: He Lacks Basic
Intellectual Infrastructures Across the Board
Trump Blurs and Blends Life (His Life)
With Media and Movies
Trump Has Scrambled Eggs For Brains
Trump Has Very Thin Conceptual Underpinnings
For His Verbal Diarrhea
Trump Forgets What He Said the Day Before,
Even the Hour Before, Even Minutes Before
Trump Is That Strangest Thing: a Pathologically
Thin-skinned Verbal Abuser
Trump's Everything Is Transactional
Trump's Language Is All Contextual Manoeuvre
Trump Seems To Expect the Authority Accorded
To a Great Writer: But Rather Than Words,
He Has Built His Achievement on . . .?

Trump's Prissy Outrages Are Punctuated by
Immature and Meaningless Phrases Like
"It Shouldn't Be Allowed" or "Hoax"
Trump Fills His Tweets With Odd Capitals and
Immature Teenaged Punctuation Mistakes
Like *!!!!*
Trump's Claim That ISIS Was Defeated Now Reveals
Him As a *Truly Dopey Fucker*
Trump Is Interested in the Exercise of Power Not
So Much For What It Achieves As the
Attention Its Demonstration Brings
Trump, Like Freud's Vienna, Combines Almost
Perfectly the OTT Gentility of NYC
"Society" (His Mother) and the Cesspit
Business Activities of Patrilineal Sewer Rats
(Grandfather and Father): He Is, in This
Sense Too, a True "Big Apple" Gangster
(As in *Goodfellas*)
Trump's Talk Ejaculates Like One of Those Guys
Who Doesn't Care Where It Lands
Trump Can – It Can't Be Denied – Be Very
Gangster-funny
Trump Loves Chaos, and Loves To Use It

Trump Is Lucky
Trump Is a Braggart
Trump Hates Real Intelligence With Canniness
Trump's NYC – Like Woodard's "New Netherland"
– Combines Perfectly Social Liberalism
in *Mores* With Extreme Social Viciousness
Trump Lifts the Old American Penchant For
Boosterism, Self-interested Exaggeration
and Bloated Celebrity To a New Level
on the Fantastical Shelf
Trump Now Talks Like an Evangelical Whose
Lord-speak (i.e., Himself) Is Always Rosy,
Glorious and Triumphant
Trump's Plan For Bibi-dom Is Like a Bad Poem:
No One Takes It Seriously Except the Author
and His Zionist Lickspittles
Trump's "State of the Union" Was Yet Another
Momentary "State of the Self", in His Self-
identification With the Nation

FINAL REPORT?
(A WORK-IN-CONTINUOUS-PROGRESS)
(2020)

Trump Is Often Strangely, Aggressively "Camp"
Trump Will – Sooner or Later – Be Run Out of
Town Like the Duke and the King
Trump Is *Bully, Bully, Bully*
Trump Is So Shallow That He Has No Real Sense
of the Depths Under the Reflections of His
Beloved Narcissus
Trump (of Course) Does What He Claims Others
Do: a Key Technique To Obfuscate His Own
Malfeasance
Trump Is Corrupter-in-Chief
Trump Fears Above All That Russian *Kompromat*
Trump Must Always Be *Deciphered*
Trump, Donald John, Is a *Don* (So *Don* Is a *Don*)
Trump Is Full of Narcissistic Whims and Desires
Trump Now Literally Calls Himself "The King":
Who Is Now (Donald's Own Words)
"Emboldened, Focussed and Triumphant",
Dealing With "Grievance, Persecution, and
Resentment"
Trump Represents Pure, Unadulterated Belief:
Like My World-wandering Arkansas
Waiter Who (Asked *Why*) Said Simply:
I Believe in Him
Trump Always Needs To Say It Out Loud: It Cannot
Be Left in the Non-existence of Silence

Trump Is My Bronxville (Westchester) Childhood:
Total Suburban Entitlement, Deviance, and
Viciousness of the Bullying Whiting Family
Trump Is Corrupting All Around Him (People and
Structures) So As To Better Unleash His
Drive For Total Control

Trump Legitimizes
Trump Weaponizes
Trump Is a Tacky Gatsby Bamboozling the
National Nick (We've Read It All Before!)
Trump Is Treacherous
Trump Is Treasonous

Enough of Trump for now, says Huck on his high wire

Nota Bene, *African Americans:*

Trump Is Whitey
Trump Loves Those Good Ol' "Black Codes",
Though He Hardly Knows It
Trump, "The Copperhead": *Viper, Rebel, Traitor, Scalp*

Into the Pandemic!

Trump Is Base
Trump Is Petty
Trump Is Pure Ideology of Self
Trump Is Psycho-Panglossian in
Deep Self-interested Denial
Trump's Bearded Son's Virus-rant Reminds Me of
Yugoslavia in the Late Eighties
Trump Dumps on Human Beings

Trump Attacks and Mocks Anything and Everything,
However Reasonable or Justified, That
Threatens Him Politically or Personally,
Even the Virus
Trump Is Crazy Batshit
Trump Is the Diametrical Opposite of *Arete*
(Greek Sense)
Trump's "Planning" Is Utterly Haphazard,
Lackadaisical, Erratic and Chaotic
Trump's Deepest Root Is Profound Envy of
Anybody or Anything Better
Trump Himself Personifies "Hack and Fake",
Misinformation and Disinformation

Trump's "China Virus" Trope Reveals a
Vicious Central Spot That Watermarks
His Whole Psyche
Trump – Like Us All To a Degree, But To His Own
Nth Degree – Is So Trapped in His Past
Behaviour-and-speech That It Would Be Still
More Frightening If He Tried To Flee It
Trump Has Quite Consciously Cultivated a
Personality Cult: Fascinatingly Easy
Trump's Special PR Brand of *Bizzarrie*
Combines Fabrication, Attack and Insult
Trump's Orangey Marsupial Look – *Bronx Colors*
Brand? – Is Likely Self-slathered Make-up
Aimed at Covering Rosacea on Pallid Skin:
Like J.P. Morgan's, or Ancient Pistol in
Shakespeare
Trump's Coloured Face Is, Therefore, a True Mask,
Both Physical and Psychological
Trump's Regular Misreading of Others' Words,
Gestures and Grimaces May Suggest Masked
"Neural Diversity", As Do His Verbal
Repetitions and Fillers
Trump's Attempts at Virus *Gravitas* ("We're at War")
Suggest a Louche and Slovenly Mind That
Simply Structures Itself This Way
Deliberately

Trump Often Enunciates Certain Words Slowly and
With Duck-like Lips As If Contemptuous of
Their Meanings

Trump Is Actually a Crappy Manager,
a Total Apprentice, We Now See
Trump's Spin Cannot Impact (For Once) the Virus,
Which Doesn't Give a Fuck About It and Has
No "Base" But the Human Body
Trump's Huckster "State" of the Union Speech Will
Be Seen As the Height of Hubris: True Pride
Before the Fall

Trump Is, For Sure, "Neurally Diverse"
Trump Has No Concept of How the Memory of
His Presidency Is and Will Be Constructed:
He Is Mr All-Here-and-Now,
a Form of Deep Insecurity
Trump Is a Degenerate Descendant of the
"Creole Nationalist", in Benedict Anderson's
White Colonial Sense
Trump Is Pure *Pulp Fiction*

Trump's Grandfather's "Westward Ho!" Is Part of a
Formation That Leaves Every Skeleton or
Broken Wagon Wheel Behind, on the
Glorious Trek To Future "Paydirt"
Trump's Anti-malarial Quack Virus-fix
Demonstrates He Is a True Snake-oil
Salesman: a Tangled Psychology of Total
Self-belief, Evangelical Certitude
and the Mighty Dollar

Trump-ness Is Cognate With Numerous
Latinate Nouns
Trump Demands Praise, Fealty, Attention,
Dis- or Misinformation, and on and on
Trump's Ingrained Warp Is Iago's Envy?
Trump's True Inner Wasteland Is Punctuated
With the Gaudy Prayer-flags of These Lines
Trump Is NYC Debutante Élite Privilege Gone
South (Literally)
Trump's Foolhardy Arrogance Is Best Expressed by
His "Faith" in Gut Instincts

Trump, in Short, Is a Bitch (Non-gendered)
Trump, As Spin Performer, Is Running Up Against
Deadly Seriousness
Trump Is a Total Control-freak Apropos Power
and Discourse
Trump's Vast Ego Is an Insecure Ego
Trump's Most Ridiculous Description:
His "TOTAL" Control of Lockdown
Trump Has the Contempt of the Colonial *Criollo*
For *Peons*
Trump Plays Politics With Everything, As a Form
Also of Self-exculpation

Trump's Deepest Media Addiction Is a
True Craving For Anti-solitary
Combativeness in the Limelight
Trump's Deeper Delusional Streak Is
Quintessentially Western: It Is Widely
Shared by a Populace Fed on the Pabulum
of Advertising, Social Media, Therapy-speak,
Groupthink, Newspeak, Doublethink
Trump Embodies the Often Highly Rude,
Aggressive, Vituperative Style of
New York City Street "Manners"

Trump Has Assembled an Anti-scientific New Model Army of Political Ideologues, Evangelicals, Anti-vaxxers, Hippie Detritus, Conspiracy-theorists, Self-deemed Losers and Begrudgers, Ranters, Grifters and Reckless Wingers …

Trump Is an Expert in Winging It, Like All Con Artists

Trump's Thinking on the Virus Is Essentially, at Core: *Hotel, Hotels, His Hotels*

Trump Is Ivy League Spoilt Entitlement Gone South

Trump's Bizarre Lingo – *Beautiful, Wonderful, Incredible* – Is a Gangster's Self-affirming Filler

Trump Has Literally No Sense of the *Corrupt:* Hence His Brazenness

Trump's Mortal Fear of Humiliation Is a Sure Sign of Insecurity

Trump Wallows in Overwhelming Complacency

Trump: New Yorkers Intuitively Understand This Hamster-like Gangster

Trump Is "Just Crazy", Like Some Mobster Nero

Trump Is Impossible To Imagine As a Scuba-diver
Trump Is Permanently Off-the-cuff,
Unable To Think Clearly Before Speaking
Trump's Personal Dislike of Blood Reminds Me
of Hitler's
Trump's Fear of Wearing a Mask Is Fear of Mockery:
Hence His Sense of Eternal Strength,
Masking Vulnerability
Trump Tends To the "Cultic" in Order To Avoid
Structural Challenge To His Delusional
Psychology
Trump Has (or Will Have) a Secret Virus Weapon,
Like Hitler and His V2
Trump's Adolescent Language – "Warp Speed",
"Super-duper" – Is More Lazy Complacency,
Suggesting Thwarted Intellectual
Development
Trump Uses *Doublethink* in the True Orwellian Sense:
the Resultant *Doublespeak* Helps Him Shoo
Away the Cognitive Dissonance of Reality
Itself
Trump's Doublethink Is Evident in the Bifurcation
Between His Formal White House
Statements, and His Personal Actions
and/or Tweets

Trump Is Surrounded by Quacks of All Sorts
Trump Does Whatever He Wants
(and Has Done Always)
Trump, Like Many Hamster-gangsters on Their
Rodent Wheels, Relies Heavily on
"Knowledge" Acquired Orally
Trump's Denialism (Realities, Vaccines, Scientific
Facts) Is a Sure Sign of Cultic Thinking

Trump Has Become The Great Cultural Warrior
Trump Descends, Via Grandfather, From Old West/
Wild West Origins
Trump Has Created an Internal National Ideology
Unmatched Since McCarthyism's
External Threat
Trump, It Must Be Allowed,
Has Real Outward Armature
Trump Is Master of *Bravura* Bravado
Trump, Like Those Bunyan Blimps of Him,
Is Literally Bloated With Celebrity

Trump Is a Mischievous Beelzebub, *Baal of the Flies*
Trump (As Here) Is a Retarded Rubik Cube
Trumpism Is Already Cult-and-idol

Trump, Like Stalin, Is Trapped by History,
His History
Trump Is Now a Runaway Wrecking Ball
Trump Is a Deep Extremist
Trump – From "Birthers" To "Postal Ballots"
– Tells the Same Rigged Story
Trump Will Be a Disaster For Both the Union
and the Republic
Trump Is Decades of Watched Media Rot
Trump Will Try To Steal the Election
Through Flaws in the System
Trump Is 1967 Unreconstructed: "Loafers" With
White Socks, Missing the "Summer of Love"
Trump Is Now Totally Out of Control

Trump's Threatened Use of the Military May Lead
To a "Constitutional Coup", Since Their
Serious Oath Is Not To the Commander-in-
Chief, But To The Constitution Itself
Trumpian Fever Continually Reminds Me of the
Civil War Build-up of the 1850s
Trump Has No Concept of Responsibility,
Which Requires Finally a Certain Empathy
Trump, the Psychological Tyrant, Loves To Master:
Is Indeed "the Master From Amerika"

Trump Striding From the Plane in *The Apprentice:*
Such Media Dreams Are "His Locus of
External Verification", As a Therapist Might
Call It
Trump Loves, Is Addicted To, the Sound of His
Speaking: Much More Important Than Any
Agency or Action That Flows From It
Trump Is an Inflamer and Weaponizer
Trump Is a Mobster Dr Jekyll and Mr Hyde
Trump Is a Chaos Work-in-progress

Trump Has Resurrected the Bull Connor Shite, Only
a Stone's Throw From That of Bull McCabe
Trump, Using the Word "Dominate", Let the Cat
Out of the Bag
Trump Always, Somehow – at the Key Speech-
moment – Defaults To "Hucksterspeak"
Trump Is Perfect For the Malcolm X Meme,
The White Man
Trump Knew Exactly the Subtext of That
Miami Police Chief's Cracker Quote
(*When the looting starts, the shooting starts):*
White Naïveté To Think Otherwise
Trump Is Beginning To Fulfill Baldwin's Prophecy:
The Fire Next Time
Trump Is Becoming *Belfast Redux*

Trump Just Loves the Self-confirming Sound
of His Own Voice
Trump's Politics Are a Gross Form of Vulgar Marketing

Trump's Rage Is Loser Rage
Trump's Fury Is His Secret Lack of Success
Trump's Iconography (or Parody) of Patriotism –
Flags, Pins, Bibles, Tweets, Rants – Somehow
Always Lacks the Felt Authenticity of a True
Conservative
Trump Just Can't Be Nice or Self-aware
For Any Length of Time
Trump Has Mental Health Issues (For Sure)
Trump Is Needy
Trump, Like All of Us, Is the Sum of All His Choices
Trump's Hair Sits on His Head Like a Windblown
Frisbee

Trump Is Cry-Baby-in-Chief
Trump's Image of a "Strong Person"
Is Actually That of a Weak Person
Trump's Many Manias, It Is Now Clear,
Have No Rock Bottom
Trump, Sniffing a Rotten Order, Is "Defining
Deviancy Down" (Daniel Patrick Moynihan)

Trump & Sons Have Embraced Explicitly,
By Using the Word, "Magical" Thinking

Trump Most Likely Will End Badly
Trump's Final Political *Götterdämmerung*
Might Just Conceivably Blow Us All Up

Trump Is a Race-baiter
Trump's Eternal Conflict Is "Losing the Room"
Trump's Loss of NASCAR Over the Race Issue
Is Highly Significant
Trump's Alienation of the Military Is Well Under Way
Trump Is Pathetic
Trump Is Running Up Against a Deep Younger
Cultural Shift on Race, Even Amongst
Conservatives
Trump Is Dwarfed by the Instinctive Popular
Understanding of the Trauma
of the Civil War
Trump Is Loyal To the Stupid
Trump's Aides Are Becoming More and More
Like a Mobster's "Associates"
Trump's Reference To "My African Friends"
Has All the Credibility of a Mobster's
Embrace of Fair-weather "Friends"

Trump May Now Have Early Alzheimer's

Trump, Like the "Slave Kings of Yore", Mounts His House Party While Mere Slaves Die in the Fields: It Is the Same Psychological Story

Trump's Hucksterism Is Striking For Its Neediness

Trump's Talk of Too Much Testing Is "Denialism" Pure and Simple

Trump's Use of "Bad": Mob Word For Self-interest

Trump's Moderation Is Always Put on: His Scripted Veneer For Ranting White Supremacy

Trump Is a *Modern* Confederate, Like the Dixiecrat Battle Flag Now Commonly Displayed

Trump's Relation To Rock or Pop Music Is More "Partial Identification of the Ego" Vis-à-vis the Media Moment: How Else Explain the Madcap Idea of Sending Elton John's *Rocket Man* To Kim Jong-un

Trump Uses Lawyers Like Mobsters Do

Trump's Key Thing Is To Express:
Saying More Important Than Doing,
That Old Huckster Tradition

Trump Speaks Out of Both Sides of His Mouth

Trump's Take on the Virus Is Rather Like Stalin's on the Ukrainian Famine

Trump May Simply Refuse To Leave The White
House (Aptly Named)
Trump's Predictions Are Always Crazy
Trump's *Fantasia* Speech on the Fourth of July Was
Pure Self-description, Pure Transference
Trump Is Continually Speaking Two Ways: "The First
Phoney" To Cover "The Second Real"
Trump, at the Huckster Centre: *Me* Using the
Language of Secularist Salvation
Trump Represents a Real Attempt To Rejuvenate the
Spirit of the Confederacy: The Very Thing My
Great-great Grandfather Hunted Down With
His East Tennessee Mates

Trump Is a Self-glorifying, Self-pitying *Loser*
(a Word He Hates)

Trump (Mary) Confirms What Has Long Been
Obvious: That Uncle Donald Is Deeply
Unwell, Both Emotionally and
Psychologically
"Trump's Filter Bubble", It's Now Clear,
Will Prove a House of Cards

Trump, a True Symbol of Hate,
Thus Calls Others the Same

Trump and the Phrase *Appreciative of the Basics*
Amount To *Chalk and Cheese*

Trump Is Pure Distraction, Both As Tactic
and Content

Trump "Pisses Ice" (Roy Cohn, Who Should Know)

Trump Is Lining Up Conspiracy Theories,
Like Q-Anon, For the Election

Trump's Continuous Neediness For Affirmation
Is Unregulated, Unmoderated, Unevolved

Trump, Strange To Say, Is Fragile

Trump Is a Different American Species, Highly
Secretive, and Largely Unstudied Till Now
by Self-absorbed, Self-satisfied Liberals

Trump's Bubble-clash With the Globe
Is Now World-historical

Trump Is a True Master of Insulting Humour
and Nicknames

Trump, To Use His Own Lingo, Is a "Nut-job" and
"Mental Case"

Trump, The Zero-sum Leader:
Truly His Own *Nonesuch*
Trump, in Fact, Is a Nothing, a Zero, a True Cipher
Trump Is an Organic Confederate,
Though in Much Else a Chameleon
Trump, As Snake-oil Salesman, Must Always Stick
With the Present Moment, the Moment of
the Sale: What Happens To the Snake-oil,
or the Pandemic, Is Eternally in the Future
Trump-the-Grifter's "Mark" Is *We the Mob*
Trump Sells Himself: That Is, the Illusion-delusion
of Himself
Trump *Talks Up, Talks Up, Talks Up*
Trump the Showman Is the Prima Donna of
His Own Drama
Trump's First Pandemic Strategy Was To Make It
Sidebar To His Tissue of Lies, Diversions
and Circuses
Trump's Meeting With "Ali G":
One Fraud Instantly Knows Another

Trump Always Copied and Cheated
Trump Is Messing Now With the American
Federation: Think *Yugoslavia*
Trump's Early "Innocent Hyperbole"
(The Art of the Deal) Has Now Metastasized

Trump, in the End, Will Ditch All the "Greenhorns
and Flatheads" Trashing His Vacated
"Cameleopard" Con, *The Royal Nonesuch*

Long live Jim (especially) and bravo Huck!

Viva *Samuel Clemens!*

Trump Is Spread-eagleism Resurrected and Run Riot
Trump Is Today's "Peace Democrat"
Ranting Against Lincoln
Trump Loves the Rôle of Character Assassin
Trump's Future *Statue-in-mind*
Has Already Been Pulled Down
Trump's Final Demise Requires a Big White Fight
Trump's Use of the War-word *Surge* Is Code For
Militarizing the American Street:
External Empire Come Home To Roost

Trump Is Seeking, First Direct Decree Powers,
Then Emergency Powers
Trump May Actually Attempt To Engender a
Semi-conflict With China
in Time For the Election

Trump Aims To Dynamite Social Trust:
Part of His Malign Playbook
Trump's Heroes Belong Mainly To Tyrannies
Trump Is Everywhere Engineering Conflict
For the Election: Partial *Martial Law*
Now Conceivable, Allowed Under The
Constitution and With a Long
Federal History
Trump's *New Nice* at "News" Conferences Must Have
Been, Inwardly, a Self-torture of Houdini
Proportions
Trump Is Something Out of Kubrick's
American Weird
Trump Has Uncorked a Pandora's Box of Words
and Therefore Actions
Trump, Psycho-socially, Is Rat Poison
That Requires Rat Poison

Trump Is a Political Sniper
Trump's Ammunition Is Twitter
Trump Is a Wacko Ahab Hunting Always For
"The Great White Way" (His Own)
Trump Has Commandeered *USS Pequod*
Trump Finds *Thinking* Simply Too Much Work:
Golf Is More Fun

Trump – Unchecked, Re-elected – Is a Clear and
Present Harbinger of Much Worse Danger
To Come

Trump Is a Beacon of Malevolence
Trump, Donald John – As a Name – at Least Lacks
the Comic Strip *Junior*
Trump's Fucked-up America Might Be Still More
Fucked-up by This All-American *Mr America*
Trump, Oddly, Brought *Miss America* To Moscow's
Miss Universe: But Why?

Trump is Cracker-jack Jacksonian
Trump Is Vicious Suburbia
Trump Is a Destroyer of Norms and Institutions
Trump Is a "Malignant Narcissist"
Trump Will Over-Trump
Trump the Huckster Needs To Talk Over:
In Order To Latch Onto His Phoney Facts
Trump Is Not the Pre-1970s Old WASP Order
in Manhattan
Trump's Lies Are Rooted in His Many Angers
Trump's Foray Into Golden-hued Numismatics
Proves Once and For All What He Is at Base:
a Cheap Carnival Barker

Trump's Blunderbuss (Portland Makes Clear)
Could Trigger a Scattershot *Irish Trouble*s
Across the Continent
Trumpism Is an Authoritarian Personality Cult

Trump Is Now Clearly Mentally-emotionally-
constitutionally Unfit For Office
Trump Is the Created Creature of *Rupert the FOX*
Trump's Chaotic *White* House Is Engendering,
Engineering and Feeding the Coming Global
Chaos ...

Long Live Malcolm X!

Viva *James Baldwin!*

*To be continued, says republican Huck
on his high Irish wire ...*

---

*Belfast, or Béal Feirste
20 January 2017 – 31 July 2020*

FINAL ADDENDUM:
"Shine, perishing Republic …"
(2020)

Trump Sees Only a World of Fakery:
So of Course He Fakes
Trump Uses Doubt and Denialism Exactly Like His
Doppelgänger Putin
Trump's Bumbling Use of Paper Graphs
(Famous Interview!) Suggested Both
Inattentiveness To Huckster Props, and Some
Vestigial Respect For a Flunked Education

Trump *Père et Fils* Have Clear Literacy Issues
Trump's Rhapsodizing on the Mystery of *Wind*
– *I never understood wind* – Suggests
Refreshingly (at Least) a Crackpot Poetic
Neurodiversity
Trump Has Tough American Surface-confidence
of Earlier Periods
Trump Is Like a Seventh-grade Rich Dummy
in Bronxville

Trump's Pretext of Inauguration-slight For
Non-attendance at a Funeral Says It All
Trump Really Disgraces the Office of the
Presidency

Trump's Flow Is Flecked With Staggering Errors
Embedded in a Lava of Narcissism and
a Lifetime of Ignorant Readymade
Ideological Rant Like the Rich Crazies in
Bronxville Cafés: *That Woeful Culture*
Trump's *I don't know* Is a Secret Facetious Code
Directed at the Bat-radar of His White Base
Trump's Enemy Obsession Is the Alien *Obama*

Trump Often Deploys Language As a Sledgehammer
of Jumbled Fragments, So As To Dominate
the Moment: a Kind of Highly Disturbing
Verbal Violence
Trump Never Attempts To Shape His Speech
To Convince, or To Win Over:
That Impulse Appears Alien
Trump Has No Sense of Humour at All
Trump's Habit of Leaning Forward When Seated,
Pulling His Jacket Downwards, Feels Like a
Goodfella Power Gesture
Trump Bristles With False Smiles and Power
Gestures Infusing His Psychology:
Unbeknownst To Donald, He's Highly
Transparent

Trump Jr Is Openly Illiterate
Trump Sr Slurs Words and Phrases
Trump – in Light of the French Etymology –
Is Truly *Sur* Real
Trump Has Obviously Never Dwelt Seriously on
God or *The Bible*: For Him, Mere Shibboleths
Raised High
Trump Proliferates Neologisms – Is a World-class
Maker of Malapropisms

Trump's Love of That Odd Word *Hoax* Proves
Self-revealing: Likely Derived From
Hocus-pocus, a Magician's Incantation Over
Sleight-of-hand, Itself a Form of "Pig Latin"
Trump Is Now Literally "The Greatest Show on
Earth" *(Ringling Brothers and Barnum & Bailey)*
Trump Has So Little Inside, He Must Bloat With
Celebrity
Trump's Hoaxing Is of a Piece With the Salem Witch
Trials: That First Hocus-pocus Descending
from Glanvill's Book Via the Mathers, Father
and Son
Trump's Historical Significance, in Part:
Old Showman Meets New Social Media

Trump's (Self-) Description of Others As "Nasty, Mean, Horrible" Is Truly Delusional Hypocrisy High on Rat Poison

Trump Aims To Make of the Federal Government His Tammany Hall, With Boss Donald at the Head

Trump Has Begun "The Harris Birther Resurrection"

Trumpian, As an Adjective, Represents the Will To Belief Over All Fact

Trump Is All About the Lack of True *Education*

Trump Has Created a Fanatical Cultural Base Indifferent To Facts

Trump Would Write – If He Could, Which He Can't – Not So Much *The Education of Henry Adams,* as *The Education of Donald Fountleroy Duck*: That Whitey With a Temper, Renowned For His Semi-intelligible Garble and Wacky Behaviour

Trump Is Cheap Sixties *Jell-O*: Now Set and Hardened, With Bits of *Canned* Fruit For Ideas

Trump, in the "Clockwork Orange" of Washington Politics, Is Most Definitely the Droog *Dim*: "Dim Being Really Dim" ...

Trump and Subtlety Belong To Parallel Universes
Trump Is Simply "Not Across the Detail"
With Anything But Self-promotion
Trump's Is a Bully Bulldozer (*Doobi* Model)
Trump Has the *Empathy Gap* To End All
Empathy Gaps
Trump Doesn't Know What He Doesn't Know

Trump Defaults To Sleazy and Smooth Surface-
speech: a Kind of "Gangster Grease"
Privileging Immediate Ease of
Communication
Trump Wallows in the Uncontrolled Ego-fulfilment
and Belief-borne Denialism Now Increasingly
Characteristic of the West
Trump Is Ten Times Worse Than Nixon
Trump's Clever Use of Pardons Shows Up
(Indeed, Trumps) Obama: Why Not,
One Wonders Now, a Nod To Those
Black Panthers Still in Prison?

Trump Now – With His Characteristically Evasive,
Implicit and Incentivizing Language –
Openly Supports Q-Anon

Trump Is Not Just "Trump": He Is the Corrosion of Non-institutional *Education* (That Is, *Culture*) Engendered by "The American Free Enterprise System": Decades of Tabloid Print, Rotten TV, Advertising and Marketing, Individualist Narcissism, Unzipped Internet, Ideological Fixations and Evangelical Salesmanship, Flaky Therapies, *Woke* Excesses, and So on and on

Trump Is Our Tyrant-in-waiting

Trump Is Corrupting Bureaucracy's Internal Rule of Law, by Initially Suborning Key Federal Inspector Generals

Trump May Actually Precipitate a Deep-state Rebellion, Fulfilling His Own Conspiracy-fantasy

Trumpism Does Not Know What To Do With the Non-libertarian Idea of *an Effective State*

Trump Is a Social-media Flamethrower: the Dems Are His Japs

Trump Is Slowly (and Somehow Blithely and Overall) Suborning the Whole Federal State

Trump Is Blowback From Obama's Neo-liberal Failure (With Congress) To More Than Tinker With Systemic Change

Trump's Handling of the Pandemic Reveals, Once and For All, the American Delusion of "Freedom & Exceptionalism" Independent of Class, Race, Geography, Community

In Ireland: August and September 2020

Trump, It Seems, Has Been Briefed on Extra-judicial PEADs ("Presidential Executive Action Documents"), in Existence Since Eisenhower, With No Congressional Mandate Whatsoever

Trump's Florida Convention Was a Kind of Intellectual Horror-show "Spectacular", Somehow Reminding Me of the Stunned Kids Watching the Wife-beating Scene in *Raging Bull*

Trump's Smile Is Always a False Smile

Trump Is Able – As Was Once Said of Hitler – To Stir Up the "Inner Mask" of "National Identity" in His Followers, and So Marshall the Malign Power of This Emotional Disturbance

Trump Is Deepening the Darkening Blowback Mirroring the Excesses of PC, Cancel Culture, Victimology

Trump's Salesmanship, Like All Grifter Pitches, Aims at Belief's "Inner Conversion" To His Own Self-interest

Trump's Tweets Scare People Like Some Wild West Posse

Trump Violated the Hatch Act, at Least in Spirit

Trump's Kids (Excluding Poor Barron) – Compared To Those of the Kennedy Clan – Say a Lot About the Evolution of the Last Half-century in America

Trump's Implicit But Open Encouragement of Militias and Q-Anon Wannabe Terrorists Is Potentially More Dangerous Than Gerry Adams Ever Was

Trump Aims To Use "a Blizzard of Lies" (George Will) To Create a Mass Image of Dysfunctional American Apocalypse

Trump's Continuous Message To Supremacists: *It Will Get More Extreme*

Trump Uses Old Cold War Words *(Socialism, Agitators, Marxists, Radicals)* Sugared With Bleeding-heart Touchstones

Trump Is the Last Hurrah of Old Elementary School America

Trump Makes It Plain Subliminally:
Violence, Obviously, Is Coming
Trump Wants a Dysfunctional America: Likewise,
Many Trumpists Need It
Trump Indeed, As Much Possible, Needs Total
Dysfunction: in Effect, a Mob World
Trump Is *The China President:* a Strategy To Divert,
in Part, From Poisonous Russia
Trump Openly Supported the Kenosha Shooter
Trump Is a *Subverted Form of That Most Precious Thing:*
Alas, I Forgot What This Is
Trump Himself Is in "the Dark Shadows"
Trumpists, With Their Armed Trucks and Flags,
Have Already Lost the Urban Street:
a Key Belfast Dynamic
Trump, We Can Safely Assume, Never Read Joyce
Jacob's *The Death and Life of Great American*
Cities: "The first thing to understand is that
the public peace – the sidewalk and the
street peace – is not kept primarily by
the police ... No amount of police can
enforce civilization if it has broken down."

Trump Is Scottish Mama's Pretty Boy:
Try It in Belfast!
Trump, Unlike the Medici, Has Zero Taste

Trump Requires Damage To Do More Damage
Trump, If Necessary, Will Become a Successionist in
Spirit, Maybe Even *De Facto:* For the
"White Space", Wherever It Is in the Majority
Trump's Oft-times Comment, "We're Investigating",
Has Always For Me a Mob Vibe
Trump's Vitriolic Spewing Is High-octane Fuel For
Uncorked White Hatred and Dixiecrat
Southern Supremacy *Redux*
Trump Instinctively Aims To Make "Marginal" the
Powerful – Who, of Course, Will Be
Protected by the System
Trump Has a Track-record When It Comes To
"The Central Park Five": Shades of The
Birmingham Six, and the Same Police "Story"

Trump Is Malcolm X's "American Nightmare"
Trump Implicitly Morphs Protesters Into Rioters,
Vandals, Looters: Classic Jim Crow and
Securocrat Rule
Trumpians Would Do Well To Recall the
Pre-Troubles Police Scenario in the
Midst of Gerrymandering and Denial of
Civil Rights, Recorded by Heaney's
"The Ministry of Fear"

Trump's Support From a "Radically" and "Left"
Anti-establishment Element Verifies
Dramatically "The Horseshoe Theory"

Trump Is Orange Man
Trump Signals This: I Will Make Again the US *Us*
Trump, From His Dark Shadows, Consciously Feeds
Conspiracy Theories
Trump, Given Time, Will Attempt To Flip
Ideologically Neo-liberal Big Tech (Google,
Facebook, Twitter)
Trump Plays on Fear of Dispossession of the Old
White European Settlement by Those
Dispossessed
Trump Has "No Heart"

Trump, Echoing Jimmy Hoffa (Whom I Once Met),
Represents Corrupted Police Union Power
and Its Stuck Cultures
Trump, Most Definitely, Is an Intentional Racist
Trump's Instinctive Psycho-social Model:
Elected Dictator

Trump's Continued White House Residence (Or Not) Might Be Determined in the End by the Constitutional Oath of General Mark Milley, Chairman of the Joint Chiefs of Staff
Trump's Talk of BLM "Terror Attacks" Reminded Me Immediately of That Patriotic Nazi Phrase "Jewish Terror Raids"
Trump's Brazen Shamelessness Is a Fear of …?
Trump *Himself* Clearly Aims To Create, in Time, a Loyal "Deep State"
Trump Literally Accuses Others of What He Patently Does: *That Classic Feint*
Trump: If It Talks Like a Quack, Walks Like a Quack, Looks Like a Quack, It *Is* a Quack
Trump Is Simply and Fanatically *Loved* For His Impermeable Belief System

Trump, No Doubt (It Would Appear), Thinks He's Handsome: It's That Old White *Marlboro Man* Thing, The Way He Sets His Jaw
Trump, of Course, Doesn't "Do" Black Women

Trump Is Now Really "Off His Rocker": That Old Handmade Tennessee One We Have in the Study

Trump, the *We-the-Mob* Boss, Views His Throw-away "Associates" As So Much Sucker Fodder, If Necessary (Which Is Often)
Trump Disgraces the Dead

Trump Deep Down Values Only Transactional Life Choices: Anything Else Is for "Suckers" and "Losers"
Trump Loves It When *Others* Are *Beholden* To Him
Trump's Overweening Cynicism May Be Down To His Own "Loser Frustrations"

Trump Craps on His Family's Silver Platter
Trump, Obviously, Can't Control His Loose Tongue
Trump Fondly Imagines He Is in Line For a Nobel Prize (Or So He Says)
Trumpage and *Trumprage* Now Enter the English Language
Trump, in a Word, Is *Reaction*

Trump Must Surround Himself With Hacks, Flacks and Quacks
Trump Speaks of "My People"

Trump Can Barely Read a Speech Without Boredom,
Yet He Is a Master Communicator-manipulator

Trump Is Setting the Whole Country Up For a
Huge Fall
Trump Is "Anti-Soul" in the African American Sense
Trump Makes Clear ... *What Exactly?*
Trump Also Works the Blowback Seam From
Woke Fakes (*Cf.* Sacha Baron Cohen in
Who Is America?)
Trump and *Organization* in "The Trump Organization"
Have an Ominous Ring, When You Think
About It

Trump Is a Political Cutthroat
Trump Mesmerizes Like Mind-rot Computer Games
Trump Is the True Fruit of the Supposedly "Liberal"
Social Media
Trump Derives From the Rule and Citadel of *Money
Alone:* Prestige and Status Determine
"Winners" and "Losers"
Trump Is *The Great Inflection Point*
Trump Understands That White Grievance,
If Fuelled (Kenosha Visit), Can Only Grow

Trump Is What Twain Hated Even Then: White-supremacy "Sivilization" (Now Descended To Bannon, His Ilk and *et Al*)

"Finn", let us recall, is an Irish name, meaning "white" or "fair": as in my college friend "Chris Finn", who was fair but ginger-haired

Coincidence? No way!

And "Huck"?

That is to say, of course, "Huckleberry" – a plant used by Native Americans; or in nineteenth-century US slang, "a small, unimportant person", often in mock self-depreciation; or, hence, "the exact kind of man needed for a particular purpose" . . . as in the phrase "I'm your huckleberry"

Another coincidence? I doubt it

But there is also "Pap", Huck's father, an immutable palindrome: raging against the "govment" and its infringement of liberties; a free "mulatter" who votes in Ohio; a "p'fessor in a college" who "could talk all kinds of language, and knowed everything."

So Huck, at the decisive moment of loyalty to Jim: "I studied a minute, sort of holding my breath, and then says to myself: Alright then, I'll go to hell."

He mounts again.

Trump Is the Great American Myth of *Him*self

Trump Is an *Animal*, American Usage, As He Says of Many Others

Trump: What a Perfect Name For Trump

"Trump", As in the Dictionary Entries: "To get the better of"; "to trump a trick"; "to proclaim or announce with, or as if with, a fanfare"; "to expel intestinal gas through the anus"

In Croatia: September and October 2020

Trumped-up Paranoid Postal Fraud Is the Trojan
Horse, or Achilles Heel, For a Trumped-up
Election Night

Trump Has, Essentially, a Lawless Psyche

Trump Now Leads the Digital Cult of
"The Great Awakening",
One Spreading Rapidly Beyond Him

Trump Is an Ideological Character Assassin
("Inside Every Ideologue, My Father Used To
Say, Is an Assassin": Joan Margarit)

Trump, a Proven Liar, Has the Cheek To Accuse
a Granddaughter of Lying About Her Dying
Grandmother: Straight From the Mob Gutter,
From a True Guttersnipe

Trump, Via The Great Virus Crisis, Is Flushing Out
"The Wacky" Everywhere, Especially
Amongst Celebrities, Both Trashy and
"Quality"

Trump Panders, and Must Keep Pandering

Trump Is the Conductor (Both Senses) of
Ideological Bubbles and Obsessive
Cultural Tics

Trump Has Already Created a New Style of
Government "Business", One Likely To
Spread and Endure in "Liberal Democracies":
Petty-minded, Insult-driven, Retaliatory

Trump Has Re-defined "White Supremacy"
For Our Time
Trump Is All About the Old White European
Settlement Losing, in Future, Its Assumed
Majority
Trump, As They Say, Has "a Journey", "a Community"
and Most Definitely "a Story": All That
Wokish Facebook Shite-speak
Trump Hit (Early on) on the Need For Faked-success
Algorithms in America Since the Eighties:
Now Widespread Across the United States,
Regardless of Political Outlook (*The Human
Stain, The Talented Mr Ridley,* Jessica Krug)
Trump Is Not So Much a "Blackface" Showman
(Old Racism), As a Showman
"Orange Face" (New-old Racism)
Trump Is Commander-in-Chief of All "Insecurity
Forces": a Gathering (Yes) or Even Reunion
of, *Inter Alia*, Self-perceived "Losers",
Begrudgers and Internet Tossers

Trump Is Clearly and Intentionally Fomenting White
and Black Militias, So Reminiscent of Ireland
1912-1916: But He Should Bear in Mind
That, in So Doing, "Trump Tower" Is
Exceptionally Vulnerable

Trump Is, Indeed, "Cruel": Continual Outflow of
His Total Lack of a Working Moral Core or
Conscience

Trump's Clan (Ivanka, Jared, Donald Junior, Melania)
Have As Yet No Idea How Out-of-their-depth
They Are – in Knowledge, Culture, Experience
– in Their Wild West, Business-style
Exercise of Superpower

Trump Is Goldwater '64, Weaponized (Literally):
But They Never Went Away, You Know

Trump's "Stone" (Roger), in the Soft GOP Fruit,
Speaks the Unspeakable: Already There
Is Talk of "Martial Law" and (Soon Perhaps)
"Coup" and Violence As "Self-defense"

Trump Is So Based in the Transactional, That
My Poetical-Political Patois Here Would Be
of No Concern To Him Beyond Its Wider
Harm or Benefit

Trump Is a Kind of Warped *Vox Pop* – or Leviathan
"Bubble-net" – For Millions of Voters
With Their Bubbled (and Bubbling)
Cultural-wedge Obsessions

Trump's Constant Folding of the Real Into the Unreal Merely Reflects His Fixation on "The Moment of Sale": *Whatever It Takes To Hawk Himself*

Trump Is The Great Answer To Several Generations of Questions Known As Complexities

Trump, in His Impermeable Psyche, Can Do No Wrong Because He Can Divorce – or Is Divorced – From Facts at Will (Like an Impiously Impulsive Islamist)

Trump Is the First Superpower Leader Who Can Really Be Imagined Pressing the Button in a Fit of Pique

Trump Wishes To Sabotage a Real Election With Fakery and Is Willing To Risk a Sporadic Simmering Civil War To Do So

Trump Now Becomes, Increasingly, the *Figure Head* of the So-called "Great Awakening": Our Fake Know-nothing Cotton Mather, or Jonathan Edwards, Without a Shred of Their Learning

Trump Is the First Internet President: Eighty-Seven Million "Followers" (Revealing Big Tech Word), and *The New York Times* Nowhere in Sight

Trump Is, in Truth, The Great Retreat To
Core Belief Structures Enmeshed in
"HyperNormalisation"

Trump, Says Another (Yes) American "Refugee" To
Croatia, From Ohio, "Is 100 Percent Certain"
of Re-election (by Some Means or Other)

Trump Is Now Openly Fomenting an Actual
Scattered Hybrid Civil War

Trump Just Naturally Feels Pervasive Contempt For
All But Himself

Trump Is The Great Simplification:
Here, There and Everywhere

Trump Is the Final Confirmation of the Intellectually
Dead Cul-de-sac of Tele-evangelical Political
Christianity

Trump Is a Collective Gaslighter

Trump Is Yesterday's Man Today

Trump Is a Kind of Mental Virus:
Vaccines Needed Soon!

Huck mounts again, for more of his Voltaire act.

Trump's Use of Nicknames Always Reminds Me Somehow of BDSM: He Must Be "Top" To His Opponents' "Bottom"

Trump, Implicitly or Directly, Is a "Russian Asset"

Trump Illustrates (If Illustration Was Still Necessary) That a Considerable Portion of the American People Now Share His Criminal Mind To Some Degree

Trumpistan, Under Its *Duce* Don, Becomes Ever More Radically, Racially and Violently Disaffected

Trump Has Always Been All About His "Brand" and the Monetizing of a Rampantly Self-promoted Fame: But Now the New Presidential Infamy Is a Real Economic Loser, Even For Suckers

Trump the Fraudster, According To Charges Filed by the New York District Attorney (Before the Settlement), Was Guilty of "Systematically Defrauding Economically Marginalized and Vulnerable People"

Trump Is a Master of Licensing Deals, Including With Post-Soviet Oligarchs

Trump Speaks of "Renewed Hope" For the
"American Dream", or a "New Dream":
Thus One Realizes, With Renewed Jolts, That
All This American Dream Stuff Has Always
Been Partly Salesman Hogwash

Trump, *The New York Times* Makes Clear, Is a Serial
Scammer and Schmoozer: a Prosperity-
preacher Without Faith, a Hot-gospeller For
Himself and Secular Cash

Trumpians Will Outlast Trump, Even If Their Leader
Ends Metaphorically Like the Day-Lewis
Film, *There Will Be Blood:* "Mr Daniel?" Asks
the Servant Irishman Entering the End Scene

Trump Fails To Finish at Least Half His Sentences

Trump Simply Fails To Answer Coherently or
Straightforwardly Almost All Straight
Questions, To an Exceptionally Unique
Degree

Trump Never Finishes a Thought:
They Just Go on and on

Trump's "Answers" (If Such They Are) Are a Jumbled Swerving Demotic Mishmash of Anecdotal Snippets, Free Association, Ad-libbing Lies, Random Initiatives, Lateral Allusion, Quickfire *Goodfella* Retorts, Half or Quarter Sentences, Half-ideas, Hare-brained and Half-brained Stuff of All Sorts: All Under the Arrogant Veneer of a Dysfunctional Certitude

Trump Is *Rude, Rude, Rude: Crude, Crude, Crude*

Trump, the Bitter Ranting Ideologue: Welcome To the Very Worst of New York and Westchester Wealth

Trump, Intellectually Speaking, Is a Total Crackhead

Trump Is a Blond Bimbo (*Bimbo*, Male Form of *Bimba*)

Trump (Or So They Say) Never Drinks: But What of Possible Past Drugs and Sex Addiction?

Trump and His "Trusty" Lady (Communist Family Pedigree): "Horrible People", Why Not Just Say It – Yes, Let's Just Say It, As If Eastern Dissidents

Trump Issues Mob-like Threats on Prime-time TV
(First Debate Allusion To the 1799
Logan Act)
Trump Claims It Will Be a Fraudulent Election But
"Knows" He Will Win: How So Both at Once,
Apart From His Own Plan To Rig It?
Trump Is Doing, in Other Words, a "Hit" on the
Election

Trump, Ironically, in Face of the Pandemic, Is a
"Clear and Present Danger" To the Current
Global Economic Model Due To His Inability
To Imagine Reform or Remediation of Any
Sort, *à la* FDR
Trump the Fraudster, It Becomes Clearer Every Day,
Is Perilously Balanced on His Own Long-
term High-wire Act
Trump the "Reality" TV Guru Demonstrates –
Definitively – the Total Unreality of Much
of That Medium, Especially in the United
States, Lacking Any Mass Equivalent To the
Sterling BBC
Trump, Rather Than Fiddling (Musical Sense), Plays
an Inordinate Amount of Golf As the Nation
Sickens in Many Directions

"Trump", Truly, Is Becoming a World-wide Obsession: Overwhelming – and Maybe Unprecedented – in Its Harvest of Global Attention

Trump's Use of First Names (*Joe, Chris*) When Addressing Enemies and Opponents Has All the Trustworthiness of a Mobster Buying You a Bloody Mary or Manhattan in a Bar

Trump's Politics Is a Kind of Brutal, Dystopian and Backstreet *Song of Myself*

Trump Is the Garbage Man of Used and Worthless Ideas

Trump's Patriotism Reminds Me of the Swags and Flags of a Mob Diner Hang-out I Saw in the Sixties in Little Italy

Trump, Deservedly, Is Now Releasing a Long-stored *Schadenfreude* Vis-à-vis "America" From Across the Globe

Trump – Like Much of the Most Affluent in the "West", and Beyond – Is Basically Spoilt

Trump's Lackadaisical Covid Record, Given the Level of Testing and General Medical Security at The White House, Constitutes the Perfect Example of Total Élite Privilege

Trump Often Stalks When He Walks
Trump the Transactionalist (*aka* Escapologist) Is,
All of a Sudden, Interested in *Love*, a Word
Heretofore Unbeknownst To His Tweets, To
Say Nothing of *Solidarity:* "Going well, I think.
Thank you to all. LOVE!"
Trump, Despite All His Efforts, Could Not Wish,
Insult or Tweet Away the "Kung-flu"
Trump Conflates, Needless To Say, His Personal
Worth and His Net Worth: That Ultimate
Heresy, Whose Primitive Algebra Scorns the
Weak and Vulnerable As Essentially Failures
Trump Is the Poor Man's Version of Golden Wealth

Trump, It Might Be Said, Experienced an Attempted
Assassination by the Virus
Trump, Unlike Hitler, Is Probably Less Extreme
Than His Very Hard Core, Though He Incites
Them With Hitlerian Aplomb – and So
Far, Likewise, Appears To Have No Nadir in
the Circumstances of the Given System

Trump (Mary) Is the One To Watch: She Has
First-hand Empirical Experience, Including
of the Family Tradition of Suppressing the
Acceptance of Illness or Disability, Viewed
As a Sign of Weakness, in a Way Common in
the American Past, As I Myself Experienced
Early On

Trump, Through His Father, Is the Philosophic
Residue of Norman Vincent Peale's *The Power
of Positive Thinking* Gone Completely Septic

Trump's Self-dream, or "Immortality Project"
(Ernest Becker), Is Constantly Listing
His Ship of Being Towards
the Deranged Waterline

Trump's Acceptance of Any Failure Would Collapse
His Whole Self-perceived Life-structure Like
a Nevada House of Cards

Trump Is Both the Main Progenitor and Huge
"Victim" of Trumpian Groupthink

Trump Is the Pure Paragon of *In-civility*,
in Every Etymological Sense

Trump the Pompous, Along With Pompeo (Dug Out
of the Imperial Ruins), Are Now True
Figures of Fun

Trump's Self-image Must Be a Kind of "Inner
Exoskeleton", Immune To the Usual
Evolutionary Changes Due To Living:
His Face Evokes, in Fact, the Mask of
Some Leathery Insect, in Maybe the Sahel

Trump Well Knows the Political Value of Doctors
and Medical Reports, and May Have Even
Written One Himself Just Before His
Inauguration
Trump Is Fighting Politically For Economic Survival,
As the Money Now Abandons His
"Organization"
Trump Has Become a Kind of Salesman For the
Virus, in That He Openly Denigrates Its
Multifarious Dangers
Trump Clearly Deeply *Feels* and *Lives* (Whatever He
May *Say*) Innate White Male Superiority of
the Old Sixties School
Trump's Campaign Runs Nasty TV Ads, Even As Its
King Expresses "Love" From a Hospital Bed
And Biden Wishes Him Well, Offering
Prayers (He Says) To the Irish Catholic God
of His Formation

Trump Has Become Still More Erratic:
Something To Do With the
Experimental Drugs of His VIP Covid
Treatment, Including the Steroid
Dexamethasone?

Trump's Rose Garden Debacle Was a Super-spreader
Trump Trumpets His Utter Shamelessness
Toward All Transgressions:
Mob Culture Again

Trump Loves To Free-associate About His
Grievances, Bigotries and Hatreds:
As If Somehow This Therapeutic Method
Gives Him Creative "Permission"
Trump, the Unloved and Untended Little Boy,
Is Constantly Saying in Effect:
They Are Mean To Me
Trumpists Love It That Trump Doesn't Give a
Damn About the Historical Experience of
Native Americans and Enslaved Africans
Trump's Tactics Are Those of an *Agent Provocateur*

Trump Is Being Investigated For Bank Fraud by
New York Investigators
Trump's "Associates" Have Been Indicted Like
Nine Pins: One After Another
Trump Is the Opposite of Lincoln – an Undoubted
Racist Who Evolved Towards Republican
Principles in the Throes of War and Sacrifice
Trump, Stuck and Cartoonish, Sees Himself As
the Warring Leader of Red America Against
Blue America
Trump, Like *FOX & Friends* (Rupert's Scat),
Perforce Upholds Ideological "Family"
Over Any Real Belief in the Rule of Law
When It Comes To Those Friends
Trump Actually Trump-branded the Washington
Monument on the Night of His
Re-nomination: Incredible Guy (or Guy
Fawkes) – Incredible Chutzpah!

Trump Was and Is a Trumped-up Baby Balcony
Clown Caked With Orangey Make-up
Trump Still Hasn't Learnt How To Salute
(It's Short, Stupid!)
Trump, Lo and Behold, Is Some Kind of RNC
Evangelical-political *Ho*

Trump Is Ever Crueller

Trump Plays To Fear's Default Towards Safety and Normality

Trump and His Chief-of-Staff Meadows Are in Wholesale Denial of Basic Science and So Have Gone AWOL From the Virus Field-of-battle

Trump's Tinpot Mussolini Event – *Poor Little Sick Boy* Playing Toy Soldier on the "Truman Balcony" – and the Wallowing Joyride That Endangered His Bodyguards: All of It Piss Poor Self-salesmanship Gone Invariably Awry

Trump (Clearly Now) Has Some Sort of Narcissistic Personality Disorder: Proof Positive Was His Amazing, Unhinged Self-description on the FOX Bubble

Trump Is Addicted To the Unreality TV of His Rallies

Trump's Sudden Death Due To the Virus Would No Doubt Trigger the Multidimensional "Mother of All Conspiracy Theories", a True Phantasmagoria of Populist Ignorance

Trump Confuses Self and Media, and Long Ago Lost the Actual Ability To Distinguish Between the Two: What Was Once Confined To His Trump Tower Desk – Donald Reading Stacks of Marked Articles About Himself – Has Now Become a Pathology in the Oval Office and on Twittersphere: To Total Global Amazement

Trump Simply Can't Contain Himself: It's How He Deals With Inner Angst and Feeling Generally

Trump the POTUS Is What Happened, So To Speak, To the Sixties Comic Strip *Richie Rich: The Poor Little Rich Boy*

Trump of Course Is a Faked Macho Man, Though His *Machismo* Is Curiously Faux and Prissy

Trumpians Are Trump's Actual Therapy, and/or His Collective Therapist

Trump Supporters (in Part) Don't "Get" the Virus Because They Are Healthy and White – and Truth Is Elitist, Right?

Trump, Says Even the Former Director of the FBI, Tried To Make "each of us an *amica nostra* ... part of the same family ...", Like a Mafia-style Boss Pulling "all those present into a silent circle of assent" ... "the lying about all things, large and small, in service of some code of loyalty that put the organization above morality and truth" ...

Trump's Refusal To "Self-isolate" (Ever!), As Well As His Image of the "Flu", Are Rooted in the Libertarian Sixties: That Old White World and Its Privileged Sense of American Immunity From the Outside Globe

Trump Lies To Cover Up His Lies, Stretching Backwards Like a Hall of Mirrors

Trump's Presidential Tally of Untruths and Lies, According To *The Washington Post*, Now Stands at Well Over 20,000, and Counting

Trump's Niece Says Her Uncle Is Turning the United States Into a Macro-version of "My malignantly dysfunctional family"

Trump Loves Toadies and Terrified Staff
(Is There a Difference?)
Trump Is Beyond Advice, His Own
"Smartest Guy in the Room"
Trump, Just Like Sociopathic Daddy, Judges
Himself by What He Alone Defines As
"Success": That Tautology Has a Certain
Truth, Given His Extraordinary Rise To
Global Prominence
Trump, Via Twitter, Is a One-person Cable News
Channel, With Himself As the Audience
That Counts Above All: a Meshing of Man
and Machine
Trump Is the President of Choice For a Large Swathe
of Americans Full of Pent-up Resentments,
Gripes, Grudges, Grievances, Bigotries,
Hatreds Not Only on a Political But a Daily
Level: Seeing (and So Feeling) Themselves
in the Big MAGA Leader

Trump on a Yoga Mat: It Could Only Be Imagined
in a Spoof
Trump's Racism on All Fronts Allows Him an
Appearance of "Culture-warrior Equality":
An Angle That His Base Now Pervasively
Borrows

Trump, If Defeated, May Mount a Direct Challenge
Through the Supreme Court To the
Very Right of Congress To Certify the
Electoral College, Based on Some Mélange
of the 12th Amendment and the Little-
known (But Supposedly "Unconstitutional")
Electoral Count Act of 1887

Trumpian Rallies and Militias Are Fostering the
Virus Spread: One Calculation Here May
Be That The Disease Aids Voter Suppression
and Intimidation
Trump's Successful Election Night, If It Transpires,
Will Be For Him the Greatest of All His
"Moments of Sale"
Trump, Outside the Lived Media Moments of a Rally
or "Reality Show", Is Not a "Perfect" So
Much As a Truly Desperate "Specimen"
Trump Is a Psycho Rich Guy, OK?

Huck pauses for the last stretch and more breath, eyeing his tightrope deadline, thinking he owes it to Voltaire, Malcolm X, Baldwin, Twain – and love of Brother Jim.

Trumpians Are Now a Real Travelling Political
Circus: Complete With Intellectual Freak
Shows, Smoke and Mirrors, Staffers Who Are
Mental Misfits, Good Ol' Cracker Politicos,
Hawked Conspiracy Theories, Militia
Shooting Galleries, Legal Dodgems, Fake
FOX News and Its 24-hour Ferris Wheel,
Roller-coaster Policies, a Honky-tonk Merry-
go-round of Reptilian Operatives, To Say
Nothing of the Ringmaster's Ding-dongs
on the High Striker: All Camped in the Very
Worst Washington Swamp

Trump's Likely Threefold Response To Defeat:
Dispute – Fraud – Militias
Trump's Most Implacable Foe: The Virus
Trumpian Adjectives Accrete Like a Sandbar,
Or a Silted Soul: *Bitter, Coarse, Mean,*
Spiteful, Envious, Vindictive
Trumpian, As a New Adjective:
haywire dysfunctional utopian

Trump, Through Dog-whistling and Antifa-baiting,
Implicitly Supports (in the Half-rhymed
Words of the FBI) "White Supremacist
Violent Extremists": Militia Members,
Trump Supporters With Guns, Gun Rights
Supporters, the Whole Toxic Outflow
of the Anti-government (Sovereign
Citizens) Movement in Evolution For
Decades

Trump, Then, Is a "Neo-fascist" in Search of
Allies, As Well As a "Gangster, Pathological
Liar and Xenophobe" (Cornel West)

Trump, If He Managed To Split the Military, Could
Really Trigger Widespread Civil and Racial
Violence

Trump Has Slowly Revealed What Much of America
Was and Is, So a Truth-bringer in This Sense:
The Stream That Went Subterranean in the
Sixties and Seventies Is Now a Burst "Stink
Hole" That Trump Has Sprung

Trump's Endless Lying Is Partly Explained, As With
a Mob Boss, by His Core Underlying
Objective, Stratagem or Planned "Hit" at Any
One Moment: Peripheral Issues or Facts
Must Be Swotted Away, Masked or Dismissed
As Fake, in the Service of This Self-interested
"Trump Organization" Goal

Trump's Political Gravity Has Attracted, Like Jupiter, the Gloomy Moons of Bolsonaro, Duterte, Modi, Bibi and (in Sophisticated Chrysalis) Johnson & Cummings: With More of Them To Come Unless Decisively *Crushed*, Intellectually and Politically, in the Long-term

Trump: POTUS As Business Opportunity, Though a Failed One, Which Is Why He Is Now Fighting For His Economical Life

Trump's Presidency Has Distilled His Own Worst "Essence", or Rather "Musk": Labelled, Naturally, *Always for Sale*

Trump's First Debate Performance Points To a Pathological Rule-breaker in Everything, a Gargantuan Ego Inhabiting a Brobdingnag of His Own Perverse Contrivances

Trump's Problem With Excess, One Might Say, Is That It Is Never Enough

Trump Accusing Others of Corruption Is Like Milošević Calling Karadžić a War Criminal

Back in Ireland: October and November 2020

Trump's Rally-riff About Phoning CEOs and Ordering Them To Contribute To His Campaign, Reveals a True Fantasist, With the Beloved Crowds a Kind of Personal Fantasy-fulfilment

Trump's Reign Will Be Even Shorter Than the Twelve Years of the Thousand-year Reich

Trump's Accusation About Others Making Dirty Money Is on a Par With a Don Accusing an Anti-corruption Campaigner of Impropriety: In Fact, This Is Precisely What Is Routinely Done in Eastern Europe, So a Universal Template

Trump's African American Supporters Are Actually an Old Story, Precisely Described by Malcolm X in a Famous 1963 Speech As Arising in the Economic Differences Between "The House Negro" *(who love da Massa)* and "The Field Negro" *(who hate da Massa)*: The X, of Course, Identified With the Latter

Trump Is a Seventy-four-year-old Child, According
To His Niece Mary, "a terrified little boy",
Often Full of Unhinging Fear: So a Classic
Example of Bowlby's "Attachment Theory",
Whereby the Lack of Early Love and
Attention From Care-givers Proves Decisive
To Later Temperament
Trump, Lacking Sufficient Feeling For the Attitudes
and Experiences of Others, Simply Doesn't
Do Empathy or, When He Occasionally Tries,
Achieves Only a Weak Parodying of It
Trump May Attempt a Self-pardon in Advance
Trump Is Just Unending "Bull"

Trump Has No Philosophy, No Grand Strategy,
No Worldview: It's Just Each Day's New
Self-adventure
Trump Was Described Afterwards – by Scaramucci,
His Erstwhile 10-day "Communications"
Director, or Pinocchio – Thus:
"The fact is, he's an idiot"
Trump *Does* See That Ideology and the Rule of
Democratic Law, Like Oil and
Vinegar, Cannot Be Mixed For Very Long:
This Is Why, Exactly, He Tries To Overwhelm
the Latter With the Former

Trump in Meltdown, If and When This Comes, Will
Prove Intensely Fascinating

Trump's Definition of Fake News Is Essentially
Anything That Goes Against His Spoilt
Self-interest or Its Adjacent Endlessly
Morphing Self-narrative
Trump's "Grifter Vision": a Globe of Endless
Opportunities For Exploitation, With
Potential Suckers, Losers or "Marks"
Born Every Minute
Trump's "Beautiful" Brand Is Now Fatally and
Permanently Tarnished: So His Financial
Reckoning Now Looming

Trump's Truth, in a Real Sense, Is Anything That He
Says or Does That Serves His Pure Outflow
of Pure Individualism
Trump Is a Truly Shameless Master of "False Facts"
Trump, According To the Secret Service, Is the First
President To Request a Lock on His
Bedroom Door, Though He Sleeps Apart
From Melania: Bingeing on Burgers, TV,
Tweets and/or His Daily Coiffure
– the Ultimate in Narcissistic Quiffs?

Trump's Cat's-cradle Hand Gestures Are Well
Worth Observing, For Their Tic-like
Repetitive Mobster Power Projections
Trump's Tough-guy Mockery of Biden's Age, One
Slowly Realizes, Embodies His Stupidity,
Given the Importance of Elder Voters

Trump, I Can Attest, Is Suffused With Those
Brutalist, Half-savage New York *Mean Streets*
Undiminished Until the Sixties, and
Exemplified For Me by an Old Newspaper
Headline I Came Across Four Decades Later:
Retard Home To Close In Bronx
Trump's Use of Jared & Friends, As a Completely
Incompetent Freelance Pandemic Team
Outwith the Federal Government, Discredits
Decisively the Libertarian Delusion of
Always-superior Free Market Solutions
Fuelled by Know-nothing Consultants
and Ideologues: the Very Thing That Once
Trashed Yeltsin's Russia (I Was There)
Trump, I Suspect, Is Already Highly Regretted by
Many Erstwhile Jewish Supporters

Trump Adores Personal Hatfield/McCoy-type
Feuds, Since They Level Down, Thus
(As With All *Trumpage*) Elevating Himself
and Diminishing Others

Trump Just Can't Take Face-to-face Criticism,
Especially From Women, Because He Is a
Pathological School Bully, a True "Chauvinist"
in the Napoleonic Sense
Trump, the Rich Pretty Boy of Eighties Media,
Has Morphed Into a Face of
Terrible Reckoning, Terrible Ugliness

Trump's Use of "Fake" Is Essentially a Pre-emptive
Strike, Not Even an Approach To Truth
Actually
Trumpocalypse Republicans Are Now "Brothers"-in-
arms With the Illiberal Ruling Parties in
Hungary, Poland, Turkey, India: Nativist,
Xenophobic, Patriarchal, Authoritarian
Trump's Mad Zigzagging, Seat-of-the-pants
Policy-making Does Suggest Mary Trump's
Frightened Child, Alone and Unloved,
Insecure and Uncertain

Trump Fills the American Cold War Hole,
Where McCarthyism and Soviet Antipathy
Once Squatted: Thus Using Those
Barrel-scraped Red Herrings "Socialism",
"Cuba", "the Government", *et Cetera*

Trump's Use of a New Theme Song at Rallies,
YMCA by The Village People, a Suggestive
Quasi-gay Blast From His Pretty Boy Past,
Full of Admirable Male Solidarity,
Undoubtedly Hints at the Same
Mélange-sexuality As His Hair:
a Fascinating Reversal, Like Bulgakov's Devil
Arriving in Stalin's Leningrad

Trump, It Seems, Always Plays Golf With Male
Buddies, and Confides To Male Journalists
Only

Trump's Women: Why Do I Sometimes Think
"Beards" Veiling His Own Strange Ground?

Trump, We Can Assume (Despite the Tossed-salad,
Two-bit Mess of His Mobster Patois),
Condescends To Historical "Black English",
Shaped by Slavery and the Church

Trumpistan's Long March To Nowhere Has Been
Aided, Abetted and Smoothed Along
(Needless To Say) by the Neo-liberal
Groundworks: NAFTA; De-industrialization;
Schmoozing With Overblown Celebrities and
Flyblown Funders; Reifying Wall Street and
Big Tech; Appeasing Purveyors of Murdoch
& Co; and So on, and So Forth

Trump Appears To Have Learnt Nothing from
Yugoslavia, Notwithstanding His Nuptials:
Though the Same Might Be Said of the
Leni-like Melania, Sleek and Inscrutable As
the Onyx Sphinx Adorning Split's Peristyle,
With a Soupçon of Leninist Cheekbones
Trump the Pitchman Con Artist – the Rich Boy
Willy Loman, in His Own Sad Version of
Death of a Salesman – Will Be Fascinating To
Watch, If and When He Makes His
Demagogue's Last Stand
Trump, During Any Post-election Interregnum,
Will Still Have Extraordinary Powers:
He Can Seize the Airwaves and Internet As
Commander-in-Chief, and Has a Direct Line
To Tens of Millions on Twitter, Including
Legions of Extremists

Trump's Need To Constantly Talk Up Everything
at Every Point Pertaining To Himself,
Ultimately Evidences a Fragile and Insecure
Sense of His Long-term Life-scam, As If the
Bogus CV Is Always in Imminent Danger
of Being Blown, However Aggressively
Certain He Might Appear

Trump Has Already Made an Exceptionally
Dangerous Move Before the Election:
Refusal To Accept Peaceful Transfer of Power
in a Land Overrun With Guns, Paranoia,
Fear and Loathing, Jittery Markets
Trump's Rallies Have Been Super-spreaders
(According To a Stanford Study) Leading
To Hundreds of Deaths: He Is a Devilish
Mischief-maker, an Iago Aiming To Do Down
the Hated Moor
Trump Always Seeks, Whenever Possible, a Pound of
Flesh For Slights Inflicted and Nursed
Trump Knew the Extreme Dangers of the
Virus From the Beginning:
Woodward Has It on Tape
Trump's Theft of the Election Could Conceivably
Prompt a Partisan-style Resistance in the
Long-term

Trump Has, Over Four Years, Collectivized,
Harnessed and Weaponized Populism,
Racism, Islamophobia, Anti-Semitism,
Misogyny, White-supremacy *et Al*, Into a
Single *Fasces*: He Knows Exactly What He
Is Doing

Trump's Use of Presidential Executive Orders,
Which Have a Long Constitutional History
(Under Article Two of The Constitution),
Are Proving a Powerful Half-visible Battering
Ram For the Corruption of Long-standing
Principles Informing the Federal
Bureaucracy
Trump Sucks Dark Energy From His Crowds
Trump Is an "Evil Bastard" (Irish-colloquial),
That Is To Say, a "Bad Human Being"
(American-educated): Suggesting, For
Instance, That Syrian Refugees in the
Michigan Winter Go Back To the Warm
Climes of Their Ruined Land
Trump Is Inexhaustible, Both As Storm and Subject

Trumpists, Above All, Are Stuck in Mental Images of Historic America, Once Described Thus: "an island on a continent in a shrinking world": Alas For Them, This Vast Untenable Insularity Is Slowly Being Punctured Forever

Huck looks back for a moment, then forwards.

Trump Aims To Wall Off a Challenging World

Trump Wanted To Ditch Puerto Rico Yet Buy Greenland

Trump's Blackened Hands Are, Well, Trumpy and Wimpy

Trump's Angry Big Body Has Obscured the Frightened Little Boy, Wrapped Up Inside a Huge Cocoon of Emotional Scar Tissue

Trump's Adult Second Nature Is Pre-emptive Character Assassination

Trump Is Setting Febrile, Volatile, Tribal, Deep-rooted Cultural Archipelagoes Across the US – Universities, Business, *Rus* and *Urbs*, Histories – One Against the Other

Trump Is Eroding the American "Civil Religion" and, With It, the Roots of American Social Empathy

Trump, Says Niece Mary, Is a Tissue of Crazy-making Pathologies Whose Actual Diagnosis Would Require a Battery of Tests

Trump Is So Narcissistically Entered Into That He Cannot Face the Loss of Losing

Trump's Drumbeat of Lies Is an Ever-darkening Tattoo

Trump's Use of the Adjective *Legal* (So Implying Elsewhere, *Illegal*) in the Matter of Voting Is a Code Word For Race and Immigration: Remember, Slaves Were Legally Two-thirds of a Person in The Constitution For the Purposes of the Dixie States' Antebellum Federal Representation

Trump's Attacks, Incredibly, Mirror Quite *Exactly* What He Himself Is Doing (Fraudulence, Fakery, Lying, Cheating): Classic Offense-defense, Built-up As a Technique Over a Lifetime of Educational, Social and Cultural Failure *As a Person*

Trump Speaks a Deeply *Cultural* Language That Can
Just Sail by Any Reference To Facts or Truth:
This Is Why It Resonates With His Base
Like a Tuning Fork of Expectation and
Recognition, Born Especially of This Further:
Perceived Cognate American Cultural
Formation

Trump, Who Once Mocked a Disabled Journalist,
Was Thereby True (in Another Way) To the
Nefarious Origins of the *Jim Crow* Figure,
As Related in One Account: an Elderly and
"Deformed" Song-and-dance Slave
Ridiculed by Whites

Trump Is a Political Ponzi Scheme

Trump Is a Solipsist Who Somehow Needs a Crowd:
It's All Confession-cum-projection

Trump Neither Believes Nor Disbelieves His Lies,
So in This Sense Hardly Knows He's Lying:
It's All Huckster Utility

Trump Uses Lies and Conspiracy Theories Exactly
Like Orwellian *Doublethink* in *1984*:
Ultimate Test of Total Labile Loyalty,
Equivalent To "Being Made" in the Mob

Trump Is, in Fact, Mendaciously and Seditiously Fact-phobic

Trump Is Contemptuous, Inwardly, Like All Grifters, of *His* "Suckers" and "Marks": That Is To Say, His Grifted Base From Whom He Will Grift Still More Money, Regardless of the Electoral Outcome

Trump Constantly Speaks of How *Respected, Great, Best in History* His Current Lickspittles and Associates Are, As If There Exists Some Kind of Reputational "Neverland" Where Such Ahistorical Judgements Have Been Made and Preserved, Regardless of Common Knowledge and Basic Intelligence: It's Just More Stupid Boss Mobspeak That Needs Deleted Politically

Trump Worked Out Long Ago That There Are Many Financial Opportunities, Both "Legitimate" and Criminal, in Stirring Up the Diversions of Social Chaos, As We See in the Saint's Day Scene in *The Godfather*

Trumpian Bubbles, in the Widest Sense, Have Now Become Endemic To America and Beyond: Formed First by Fantastical Bubble-blowers, Only To Settle Down As Truth's Padded Bubble-wrap

Trump's Bonded Arm Candy (Melania) Is Simply a
Lost Balkan Hare When It Comes To
American Cultural Complexities Swirling
Head-lit Around Her: So, Wisely, She Mostly
Keeps Mum (in Both Senses)

Trump's Still-deeper Root (Amongst Many) Must Be
Envy Woven With Inner Failure: the Two Are
Often a Single Plaid
Trump, If Defeated, May Attempt To Establish
a Kind of Alt-right Alternative Presidency
at Mar-a-Lago, His *Jefferson Davis*
Southern White House
Trump's Whole Presidency Is One Long,
Vengeful, Hate-filled, Branded, Petty,
Asinine Rodomontade
Trump De-legitimatizes Democracy As a Prelude
To First Hamstringing, Then Ending It
Trump Is Seriously Seditious

Trump's Early Lack of Real Education
Led (I Suspect) To the Urgent Confusions
of the True Ignoramus, So Resulting
in a Psychic Straw-house Built
With No Genuine Mental Tools, Training or
Blueprint Whatsoever: Perfect "Preparation"
For Tawdry Kakistocracy

Trump Has Scoundrel Cunning
Trump Uses Mendacity and Race-animus (Even
in His Own Eyes) As a Means of Galvanizing
Smaller Personal Patterns of Grievance Felt
by His Followers
Trump Taps Deeply Into Large Swathes of
Delusional and Self-delusional Psycho-social
Territory in the US
Trump is "The City on the Hill" High on Ideological
Steriods and Charismatic Opioids
Trump Has *Wilfully* Mishandled the Virus

Trump, It Cannot Be Said Enough, Is Essentially a
Mobster / Organized-crime-type Figure,
Using Lawyers To Circumvent, Skirt and
Bend the Rule of Law and All Ethical
Impediments: That Is Why, As With Many
Criminal Minds, He Can Be Admired by
Some of the Disempowered For Both His
Apparent Wealth *and* His Anti-establishment,
Anti-system, Anti-swamp Gallivanting, Like
Obverse-reverse on the "Double Eagle"
So Beloved of US Numismatists
Trump, in Short, Illustrates That Gangsters Have
Always a Certain Golden Glamour and
Street Credibility Outwith the Hated Order
They Fleece

Trump May Attempt a *De Facto* Electoral Coup
Trump Is Phenomenally Dangerous, More So Than
Even His Bitterest Mainstream Opponents
May Imagine
Trump's Oval Office Is a Deranged Xanadu
Trump in Jim Crow Florida Would Have Been
Perfect Material For a Lynch-leader
Trump's Fantasy-lies Amount To a
Gangster Saving Face
Trump Truly Deserves Relentless Disambiguation

Trump's Defeat, For Me (I Must Confess), Would Feel Metaphorically Like the Milkshake Scene Ending *There Will Be Blood* ...

Huck dismounts, changes into mufti and heads home to Belfast, not far from the Hatfield Bar.

Entering his study with the Tennessee rocker and 1865 Union discharge certificate, he spins on the black humour – worthy of Kubrick – at the end of There Will Be Blood:

– "I drink your milkshake, Trump!"

– "Mr Agee ...?"

– "I'm finished!"

LIFE ON THE UNIVERSAL MISSISSIPPI

(Downstream to the Future)

Trump Dies.

"I knowed it would happen", says Huck –
then, long dismounted, remembers his
alter-ego's last line:

"I been there before."

—

20 January 2017 – 2 November 2020
Ireland – Rhode Island – Croatia

What can be said at all
can be said clearly;
and whereof one cannot speak
thereof one must be silent.

Ludwig Wittgenstein

From the Foreword to
Tractatus Logico-Philosophicus *(1922)*

Let my words knit what now we lack
The demon and the heritage
And fancy strapped to logic's rock.
A chastened wantonness, a bit
That sets on song a discipline,
A sensuous austerity.

Hamish Henderson

From the "Prologue" to
Elegies For the Dead in Cyrenaica *(1948)*